RYNO!

RYNO!

By Ryne Sandberg

with Fred Mitchell

◆ ◆ ◆

CONTEMPORARY
BOOKS, INC.
CHICAGO

To my wife Cindy, who has been by my side all the way

CONTENTS

ACKNOWLEDGMENTS

I'd like to thank the Chicago Cubs organization and photographer Stephen Green for helping me with this project. Most of all, I'd like to express my gratitude to Dallas Green and Jim Frey who gave me the chance to show what I could do, and to my incredible teammates, who make it possible for me to attain my goals.

FOREWORD

When people ask me to discuss the most complete ball player in the game today, the first name that comes to mind is Ryne Sandberg. From the standpoint of providing consistency at the plate, power hitting statistics, speed on the bases, and excellence on defense, they don't come any better than Ryno, the National League's Most Valuable Player in 1984.

As manager of the Chicago Cubs, I have come to expect all-star performances from my second baseman. The way Ryne conducts himself—both on and off the field—and his disciplined approach to the game of baseball, make him an excellent role model for any youngster.

Having spent nearly thirty-five years in the game, I've seen many talented players come and go. But I feel the best is yet to come for Ryne Sandberg and the Chicago Cubs.

Jim Frey
1984 National League
Manager of the Year

INTRODUCTION

I can hear the questions in my sleep:

- "How do you prepare for an important contest?"
- "What was it like hitting two home runs off Bruce Sutter in one game?"
- "What are the rest of the Cubs really like?"
- "What do you do when you're not playing baseball?"
- "Are you married? Do you have a family?"
- "What kind of music do you like?"
- "Can you repeat the year you had in 1984?"

From the routine questions to the absurd, it seems, I have been asked them all over the last two years. A million times. It has been my nature in the past to keep my personal life and inner feelings to myself. It has had nothing to do with not wanting to share my private thoughts and past with the fans and the media. It's just the way I am, I guess. I've been this way my whole life. And now, it seems, with all the attention I received last year by winning the Most Valuable Player Award in the National League, and the Cubs winning the division championship, more people are curious about me and my teammates. I guess I can understand that. And I sure appreciate it. And, I suppose, that is basically why I would like to share the highlights of my life and baseball career with you, the fans, in this book.

I hope I can answer most of your questions and express how much I

When the dust settles, I'm confident the Cubs will be in the running for another championship.

Cindy and I had a great time on the Cubs' Caribbean cruise, but it was made complete when I was named the National League MVP.

appreciate playing in Chicago for the greatest fans in baseball. They say that, in baseball, the fans can be the tenth man on the team. Well, that sure is true of Cub fans.

I'll never forget how I felt that day last November when I was on the Cubs' Caribbean cruise with my wife, Cindy. The call came from New York that I had been named the National League's MVP. I had figured that I might have a good shot at winning the honor, but to have someone actually tell you that you're *the* winner is a feeling that is difficult to describe. I was in the shower when the call came and, at first, I thought it might be someone playing a joke. I kept asking, "Are you sure?"

Many of my teammates were on board the cruise, along with Cubs president and general manager Dallas Green and manager Jim Frey. They had a party that night to help me celebrate. Just having everyone there to share that special day with me made it even more memorable, because those were the same people who deserve the credit for my success in 1984, and I think I would put Gary Matthews high

on that list. The "Sarge" not only takes charge of a ball club with his positive attitude and performance, but he also brings out the most in his teammates. I know that he helped me and my approach to the game. When I finally reached a personal goal of 200 hits late last season, Sarge bought me a bottle of expensive champagne to celebrate. It was a nice gesture on his part, and even though it was a personal goal that I achieved, I felt as if Gary had a lot to do with it, too. We all shared the good feelings.

Jim Frey is the one who adjusted my batting stance in spring training and gave me the confidence to swing for the long ball every once in a while. He reminded me in spring training that I was strong enough to pull inside pitches over the fence instead of constantly going with a pitch or strictly trying to keep from striking out.

The award means an awful lot to me because it means fans and people in baseball believe in me, and have high expectations the rest of my career. And I know I'm going to give it all I've got to make sure I deliver.

◆　　◆　　◆

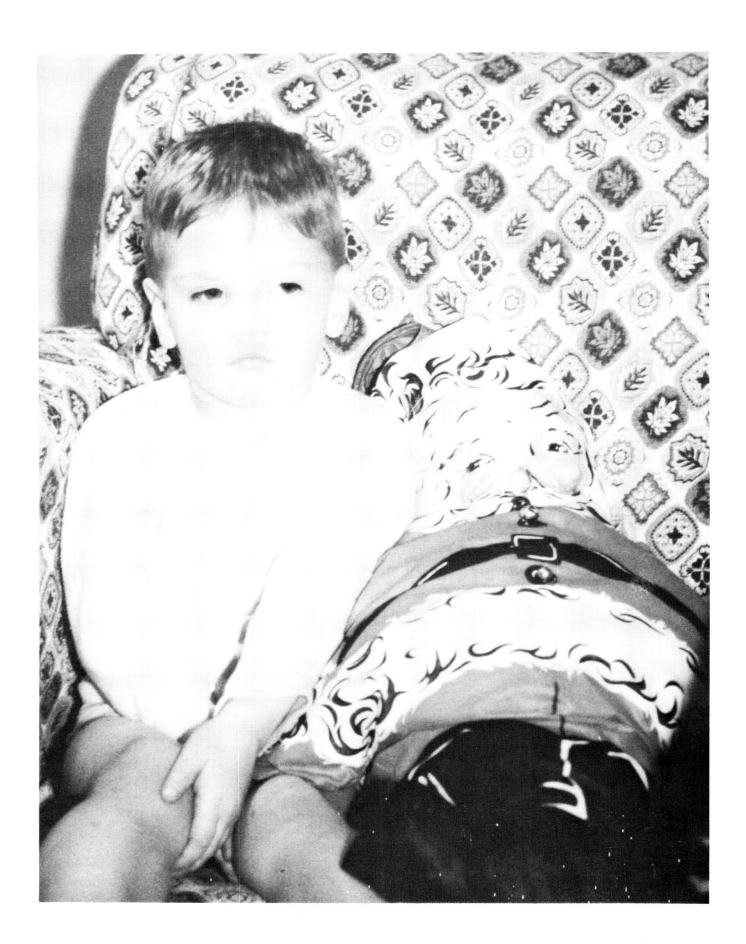

CHAPTER ONE

THE BIG LEAP

FROM CATCHING TOADS TO CATCHING GROUNDERS

I was sitting on a bench in the clubhouse at Wrigley Field playing cards with some of my Cub teammates—Keith Moreland, Gary Matthews, Ron Cey, Larry Bowa, Leon Durham, and Jody Davis—before a game this past April and my mind drifted back to how I got started in this game of baseball.

It sounds strange now, but I somehow always knew that baseball would be my profession and way of life. As far back as I can remember, it has always meant something more than just a game to me. Baseball has been my passion.

When I consider the current demands of my hectic lifestyle—playing ball nearly every day with the Chicago Cubs for nine months out of the year, traveling constantly, and enduring the perils of facing hard-throwing pitchers like the Mets' Dwight Gooden—it gives me peace of mind to think back to when I was a kid, and how uncomplicated and easygoing things were back then.

There are so many pleasant childhood memories that I cherish from growing up in Spokane, Washington. Many people say there is nothing like the great Northwest, and I have to agree with them because I know first-hand.

Many people might be surprised to find out that I had a very normal childhood, in many respects. I was just your normal kid who was really into sports. Of course, there were things I had to do as a youngster that I didn't particularly like. I think everyone can identify with that.

Ho, ho, ho! 'Twas the season to be jolly, but I don't look too happy here.

RYNO!

Before I got involved in sports, for example, I had to take piano lessons for five years from a woman named Mrs. Noble. I hated that. Especially the recitals. Now that might not sound as demanding and intense as, say, a Cubs-Mets series in September, but it felt like a pressure situation at the time.

We always had recitals right before Christmas and I could never really enjoy the holidays because I dreaded the recitals so much. One time, I remember having to play this sickening number called "Weasel Boogie." It was so embarrassing. My whole family would be there at the recitals—aunts, uncles, everybody— and there I am, MVP-to-be, playing "Weasel Boogie." Once I got involved in sports, my parents let me give up the

piano lessons, thank goodness. I don't think I can play a single note anymore.

My father always taught me to respect older people, work hard, and be disciplined. That has been my basic approach to life and to the game of baseball. So far, I guess, it has paid off. If I were to call my father on the telephone today, I know what he would

They made me wear a tie for the first time. Dan Cmos and I were named the top seventh grade basketball players at Havermale Junior High.

say. He'd tell me, "Ryne, work hard and keep your nose clean." It's his favorite saying, and it's something I'll never forget.

My family—including my older brothers Del and Lane and my sister Maryl—has been very important to me. My parents were always there to answer any questions, give me support, and help me out. I wanted them to be proud of me. I wanted them to look in the paper every day and see all the stories and the box scores and be proud that I was playing good baseball and representing the family well.

Although today my summers are filled with baseball, it wasn't always that way. As a youngster, one of the highlights of the whole year was the entire family taking off during the summer for Thomas Lake. We'd go to the same campsite and see the same people every year for two weeks, fishing, swimming, hiking, and just relaxing. For me, that was the big event of the year.

When I was about nine or ten, my main hobby was catching frogs at the lake. And every year I was sure I had caught the same one. We never marked it, but it seemed like it was always in the same place. We named it Tooly. Tooly the Toad. I'd catch him and keep him a day, then let him go. It took some strategy to catch the frogs. You had to sneak up on them and jump them quick. It was more fun catching the frogs than actually *having* them, so we let 'em go. We even caught fish bare-handed like that.

Sometimes I miss those days, and when I have an opportunity to take a

At left: A photo booth special—older brother Lane squeezed me in at Newberry's Drugstore. At right: My first visit to Thomas Lake. That's my mom.

What do you mean, it's time for another haircut?

few weeks off in the winter, I still enjoy the outdoors, whether it involves hunting, hiking, or playing golf.

These days, I like to think of myself as a well-mannered gentleman, but there were times when I was really a troublemaker. One thing we did on Halloween, I remember, was soap windows with a group of guys. Another thing that nearly got us in trouble was taking people's vegetables out of their backyards—tomatoes, cucumbers, things like that. But only when the season was right. So when people refer to me as the "boy-next-door" type, they don't know what kind of trouble they're asking for.

I grew up in a middle-class neighborhood with a big yard in the front and back where we'd play different sports all day long. We used to play our own special brand of whiffle ball. By taking plastic golf balls that were taped up, we'd practice throwing curve balls and knuckleballs at each other. We'd play all day until it got too dark to see the ball. To be honest, I think that playing whiffle ball so much taught me how to hit a breaking pitch. With the way that crazy ball jumped around, I was forced to keep my eye on the ball, and I'm sure it helped my reflexes.

When we got tired of playing whiffle ball, we used to golf in the front yard, firing shots with nine-irons over the house. We even put a flag on the hole in the back. It sounds crazy now, but we had a lot of fun. And I don't believe we ever smashed a window.

Then there were times when we had football games in the back that would take up two backyards—ours and the

lady's next door. She didn't like it very much, for some reason. I guess she wasn't a sports fan.

My brother, Del, is five years older than I am but we played together quite a bit in the early years. He didn't get to see me play any high school sports, and I kind of regret that. I'm sure he does, too. We played every sport there was together. But then he went into high school and started dating in his junior and senior years. It made me feel a little left out at first. I couldn't believe that he wouldn't take me golfing or on other outings just because of a bunch of girls. He went from doing everything with me to doing everything with girls. Then college came and he was gone for good.

My father worked long hours as a mortician and my mother worked part-time as a nurse. My mother was always the one driving the gang to the games in the station wagon. Going through grade school, junior high, and high school, she was the one who went to most of the athletic events that I played in while my father worked. The only way he was able to find out what happened was when we came home after the game and told him about it. I know it must have bothered him that he couldn't see us play.

I think I became aware at an early age that playing baseball came very naturally to me, and it is ironic that some of my Cubs teammates nicknamed me "Kid Natural." I know that being active in sports as a youngster gave me a lot of the ability that I have today. Not that catching toads helps me catch balls, but who knows?

◆   ◆   ◆

RYNO!

CHAPTER TWO

RYNO THE TYRANT

The progressions from one level of baseball competition to the next always seemed natural to me. I never felt overmatched or pressured to succeed. I played grade school softball instead of Little League baseball. Then I moved on to Babe Ruth competition, high school, and American Legion baseball. And I don't ever remember having a problem adjusting to each new level.

Everyone talks about how quiet and reserved I am now, and I can see how people would say that. But they should have seen me during football season!

It seemed like my personality changed with the sport. As a quarterback on the football team, I used to be a real take-charge guy. If my teammates didn't hustle or missed a block or a pass pattern, I'd shake them up in the huddle and holler and scream at them. I was a real tyrant. But when baseball season rolled around, I was like a different person. It was time then to take a more disciplined approach to the game.

In football, you work all week long for just one game. We had a good coach, a guy named Art Bauer, who got us emotionally charged up for every game. Once that game was set to start, I used to get so fired up that I couldn't wait to play. We had a good team and I wanted to win badly. If we didn't play well, I'd let somebody know about it. The adrenalin would really be pumping.

I lifted weights to bulk up during football season and at one time weighed more than I do now—about 190 pounds.

Basketball was my weakest sport,

There's nothing like watching the ball you just hit fly out of the park.

RYNO!

You'd be smiling too if your team just finished the season with a 22-1 record and you hit .385 as a shortstop.

I may look like a nice, mild-mannered boy in this picture, but my football teammates would tell you that I was a real tyrant in the huddle.

even though I averaged about 18 points a game. I was a pretty good shooter, but it seemed like I was never really overly aggressive in basketball. I wasn't confident about dribbling the ball, not to the point where I could dribble past guys or behind my back and between my legs. I guess I didn't put as much time into it to improve myself as a player as I did in baseball and football.

Looking back now to how those other sports helped me in pro baseball today, I'd have to say that the game of basketball improved my quickness and taught me to stay in good shape and work on keeping my legs strong. One of the things I remember about basketball is the fact that I hated the practices because of the intense conditioning involved. The practices in football and baseball were a lot of fun, but basketball was too intense. I guess that was the bottom line, even though I was an All-City and All-State player. Maybe it was the fact that it was indoors that I didn't like.

I never really had a problem juggling the three sports. They each had their own place on the calendar, and there wasn't really much of a conflict. Besides, playing three sports seemed like the thing to do at my high school, which only had about 1,000 students.

I used to take some of the losses pretty hard in high school. We had some excellent teams, and when we did lose, it was usually in the championship finals. In football, we went 11–1 and lost in the state finals my senior year. So that was a tough

loss. In baseball we were 22–1, losing in the state semifinal game. We were always one game short. Maybe it was an omen of what was going to happen in San Diego last September.

I was named to the *Parade* magazine high school All-American team as a quarterback and received some scholarship offers. But I didn't have any strong feelings about what to study in college, so I decided to sign a pro baseball contract with the Philadelphia Phillies instead of attending college on a football scholarship. I had been recruited by nearly all of the teams in the PAC 10 conference, but I just didn't feel at that time that I wanted to go to college. And I really wanted to play baseball.

There were other considerations that led to my decision not to go to college. Del was a pretty good baseball player who had gotten some interest from big

Once a quarterback, always a quarterback. I wonder how Jim Frey would feel if I brought my football onto the field.

At top: Look, Mom, whiskers! This was my last trip to Thomas Lake. At bottom: Uncle Ryno with brother Del's son, Jared. I'll make a second baseman out of him yet.

My favorite high school football receiver, Ron Jackson, and I graduated to bigger and better things.

league clubs when he graduated high school. But he decided to play baseball in college. Unfortunately, after he graduated, the pro offers sort of disappeared. He is now a high school teacher and coach.

Also, I didn't want to go too far away to college, since I had never really been away from home. So where did the Phillies send me after I signed the pro baseball contract? Helena, Montana. Not exactly around the corner from Spokane. I was miserable there for a while. In fact, I would call up Cindy (who was my girlfriend then, and is now my wife) and tell her that if she didn't come to Helena to see me, I was going to quit baseball. Lucky for me, she came.

There was a time when I wondered if I had made the right decision not to go to college. All the long bus rides, hard infields, and sack lunches! But I don't *ever* wonder anymore.

◆　◆　◆

RYNO!

CHAPTER THREE

PHILADELPHIA FREEDOM

It seems like just yesterday that I was a nervous rookie in the Philadelphia Phillies organization. During one spring training in Florida, I remember standing behind a couple of players I idolized while I was growing up— Larry Bowa at shortstop and Mike Schmidt at third base. When it was my turn to take ground balls, Bowa told me to step right in. I couldn't believe this was finally happening to me.

I was so shocked that I couldn't say a word. I was really in awe of those two guys. Now, several years later, I am beginning to feel like a veteran player myself. I feel like I can help a young player like Shawon Dunston on the Cubs by teaching him the kind of things that Larry Bowa taught me.

The Phillies tried me at shortstop and had even considered moving me to center field. I played four or five games in center field in the Florida Instructional League, and I felt very uncomfortable out there. I think they had ideas of making me an outfielder or a utility infielder, and I don't have to tell you how glad I am that it didn't happen that way.

I was traded to the Cubs along with Bowa for shortstop Ivan DeJesus on January 27, 1982. Most of the newspapers referred to me as a "throw-in" in the trade, a player who didn't figure to make a major contribution on the major league level. But Dallas Green, the Cubs' general manager and now also the president, had followed me from my early days with the Phillies' organization, and he

---

I always felt confident that I could play in the big leagues, even though some of the Phillies didn't.

15

believed in my ability all along. I thought the trade was a good opportunity for me to make the big league club with the Cubs as a third baseman or second baseman, mainly because they were bringing Larry with me to play shortstop. I played third base for the Cubs in my first year with the ball club. The next season I was shifted over to second base.

I'm second in the batting order, and Harry Caray, the Cubs' broadcaster, refers to me and our leadoff hitter, Bobby Dernier, as the "Daily Double." With Bobby having an outstanding year in 1984 and getting on base so often, it certainly made it possible for me to get better pitches. Also, Bobby is very distracting to pitchers because he's such a threat to steal. So he makes it hard for the pitcher to concentrate on me. Bobby and I go way back to the Phillies' minor league system, and even then we were able to combine for a lot of hit-and-run plays and stolen bases.

It's funny to think about it, but one of the first major league games I saw in person was one I played in. There was no major league team in my home town, so I seldom had an opportunity

I guess I have come a long way since I played shortstop for the Redding Phillies (AA) in 1980.

At top: My dog, Cleo, has come up through the minor leagues with me. At bottom: My first spring training (but not my first sunburn) in Clearwater, Florida, with Phil Thomson and other friends in 1979.

17

RYNO!

Playing next to Larry Bowa has provided me with the very best on-the-job training.

Bobby Dernier and I go way back to the minors together. That's when the "Daily Double" was born.

I've played third base, shortstop, and centerfield, but I feel most comfortable at second base.

to see a game except on television. In fact, while growing up, I saw only two big league games in person. The third game I ever saw was the first one I played in when I was with the Phillies. Before that, I would go out to see the Spokane Indians play or watch players like Bill Buckner play for the Dodgers' Triple A farm team. I guess it's pretty ironic that we ended up being teammates for a while with the Cubs.

My father (Derwent) was a great baseball fan. He never talked much about his job as a mortician and it was something we knew not to talk about. He and my mother (Elizabeth) love baseball, and I was actually named after a former Yankee pitcher, Ryne Duren. My parents told me that they saw a game between the Minnesota Twins and the Yankees and Ryne Duren was pitching. My mother was pregnant with me at the time and that's how the name Ryne came about. My brother was named after outfielder Del Ennis. My sister was the only one who lucked out by not being tagged with a player's name. I don't know of any players named Maryl.

They say that the more things change the more they stay the same. Well, things have changed for me in the sense that I am more visible to the public than I ever was before. People recognize me on the street or in restaurants, whether I'm in Chicago or in Tempe, Arizona, where I live with my wife and two children during the winter. That's nice and I appreciate the attention from fans, but I also realize that the discipline and hard work that got me to this level will help

keep me here. That's where my father's discipline and hard work speech still comes in handy.

I have received interview requests from so many different newspapers, magazines, television, and radio stations that it seems unbelievable. *People* magazine, *Sports Illustrated*, "Good Morning America"... I even posed with Larry Bowa for a spread in *Gentlemen's Quarterly* magazine. It was entitled "Double Play." It's very flattering, but, no matter what, baseball comes first.

I am generally very cooperative and understanding when it comes to giving out autographs and posing for pictures. But I have found that I cannot allow that sort of thing to interfere with my preparation for a game. I receive

PHOTO BY STEPHEN GREEN

Above: OK, kids, this is the way we do it. At right: I wear out about three pairs of gloves a week. But as long as the hits keep coming, I don't mind.

22

RYNO!

At top: Go ahead, just try to steal second. At bottom: I've always looked up to Pete Rose, but this is ridiculous.

I think you're terrific, too.

RYNO!

Playing for the fans in Wrigley Field provides tremendous inspiration. You're our tenth man. On following page: Being interviewed by Tony Kubek before an NBC "Game of the Week."

PHOTO BY STEPHEN GREEN

many, many letters, and I am considering hiring someone just to answer my mail. You wouldn't believe some of the unusual requests I receive from my fans. I have been invited to two or three high school proms. People want to invite me over to meet their friends and parents. It's really something. It's kind of funny to me, but if it weren't for the fans, where would we be? I remember being like that myself when I was a kid, trying to catch foul balls outside of the Triple A park where the Spokane Indians played.

The endorsement opportunities have increased, too, and I must say it's nice to be in a position to be able to pick and choose. My agent, Richie Bry, and

I have gotten some unusual requests. One hair spray company wanted me to do some commercials for them, but I decided not to do it. I don't use hair spray. That's not me.

I often think of my friends, former classmates, and family back home. Sports has been so much a part of my life, and so much has happened to me over the past few years, so many good things. And, I suppose, the 1984 season with the Cubs has to rank right at the top. Being named to the All-Star team and being voted the Most Valuable Player in the National League are milestones every baseball player shoots for. But you can never forget where you came from or how you got to where you are. Never.

◆ ◆ ◆

RYNO!

CHAPTER FOUR

A YEAR TO REMEMBER

Because of the recognition and attention I received from the 1984 season, many baseball fans seem to know of me only as the second baseman for the Cubs. They know about my statistics in 1984 (.314 batting average, 19 home runs, 19 triples, 36 doubles) and, believe me, I am very proud of those numbers. But there is more to me than just statistics. It just so happens that baseball is my career and it consumes much of my life. But there are other things that are very important to me as well.

I was 25 years old at the start of the 1985 season, and I often reflect on what has happened to me. I am married with two children and I'm off to a great start in my baseball career, yet I don't feel like it has all happened to me overnight. I have worked hard to achieve my goals and I think even my old high school classmates expected something special from me, whether it would be in football or baseball.

My wife, Cindy, has stuck with me through all of the rough times. We went together in high school and got married right after I signed with the Phillies organization. My daughter, Lindsey, will be three years old and my son, Justin, was born in May 1984.

Cindy and I started dating on December 23 of my senior year in high school [1977]. I knew her when I was a junior, but we didn't date. I had a late basketball game on that December 23rd night, and I told Cindy I'd pick her up at 12 o'clock midnight. I don't know what her family thought about that. I just said, "Do you want to go sledding?" She said, "Sure."

I strive for consistency in the field; defense has always come naturally to me.

The big thing at that time for the seniors was to go to Indian Canyon Golf Course and sled down the 10th hole. We'd fly for about 400 yards before we'd finally come to a stop. So that was our first date. She was fun to be with and easy to talk to. I liked people who would talk a lot to me, rather than making me do all the talking. Plus, everybody else had a girlfriend, so I figured it was time for me, too. I had only dated on and off before I met Cindy. Not anyone real serious. Little did I know that someday I would marry her.

The thing about Cindy is that I knew she didn't like me for my athletic ability or anything like that. We just got along so well because we're both easygoing and we had a lot of fun together. We went to a lot of dances together, including the senior prom. That was a pretty memorable evening. In fact, we stayed out all night. I picked her up about 6 P.M. and we went to dinner. Now, in those days, if you spent $15 for both of you, it was a nice restaurant, because I had no money. After the dance we stayed out all night with some friends and I brought her home at about 9 A.M.

After high school, we spent a lot of time together. My first year in the minors, when I played in Helena, Montana, Cindy came out for two or three weeks and stayed with me. As I said before, I was so lonely there that I threatened to quit baseball if she didn't visit me. We were seeing a lot of each other. Once I got sent to Spartanburg, she met me and the team out there and we stayed together for another two weeks. The next day we just decided to go down to the court and we got married by the justice of the peace, who coincidentally, also married Bob and Vicky Dernier. I think the whole marriage ceremony cost about one dollar. But it was worth millions and millions to me.

It was just spur of the moment. We said: "Let's go do it." We got some heat

 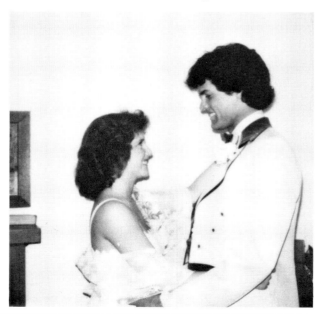

At left: Looks like something fishy is going on here with Cindy and me at Thomas Lake. At right: We're all set to go to Senior Prom. We didn't get home until 9 the next morning.

about living together, so we just thought if we got married, there wouldn't be any problem. I really needed her at that time. I was living all the way over in Spartanburg, and I'd never been that far from home. Just having her there helped me to relax and helped me develop as a ball player.

Cindy has gotten me to open up a lot, speak out, and say what I feel. If there is ever something on her mind, she comes right out and says it and everything is fine. It's nice for me to be able to do the same thing for her. She's taught me not to hold things inside. Looking back, I guess that was sort of a problem during our first few years of marriage. I was 19 and she was 18 and I guess there was a lot of growing up to do.

All the time Cindy was growing up, she was saving money. The first couple of years we were married, we went through that money like it was water. We were living off the savings she had plus the little I was making. I made $500 a month that first year at Helena. The next year it went up to $600 a month. By the time taxes were taken out and the rent was paid, there wasn't much left. So she helped out a lot.

My first year of pro ball, we lived in the back room of a house that some guy owned. He just liked the idea of letting a ballplayer live in his house. I remember having to walk four or five miles to the ballpark because I had no car or any transportation. In Helena, in the summertime, it was often 100 degrees, so by the time I walked all the way to the game and all the way back home later on, I was exhausted. So when Cindy came out to stay with me, her car really came in handy.

Cindy and I are both Virgos. Maybe that's just a coincidence. We're really opposites, but sometimes, when I read those horoscopes in the paper, they seem to fit me perfectly. I like to be neat, but not overly neat. I have high expectations for myself. All those

At left: Here's an autograph I volunteered to sign—our marriage certificate. At right: Even being married a year, we were still trying to get our heads on straight.

things that are supposed to be characteristic of Virgos are traits I have.

When I played winter ball in Venezuela, I don't think I would have made it down there without Cindy. It's tough to go down there and spend three months away from home. Bobby Dernier was down there, George Vuckovich (now with the Indians) and Atlee Hammaker (of the Giants) were down there. Ruben Amaro (now a Cubs coach) was the general manager. The manager was Bobby Wine. We had to spend Christmas and New Year's there. It was important for me to go and get some experience at playing different positions.

It was really an experience being in a strange country, but at least I understood the language. Cindy and I both took Spanish classes in high school for two years. At the time, we were asking ourselves: 'Why are we taking Spanish?' I guess we mainly

took it in case we went to college so we could have the requirement out of the way. I just messed around in the class and got by. Then all of a sudden, we're down in Venezuela and I understood what they were talking about. It came in handy.

There wasn't a whole lot to do in Venezuela except play ball and lay out around the swimming pool. There was no entertainment. There was one restaurant that served Chinese food every night. The native restaurants weren't too appealing to us. But it was an honor just to be there in Venezuela. You had to be invited. If you were invited, it was like they considered you a prospect and they were high on you and they wanted you to get some experience so you could move up to a higher minor league level when you came back to the States.

Most of the players down there were either Triple A or major leaguers. Once I got there, they already had

Cindy's been with me through it all, from the early days in high school to all the good times now. At right: The Sandbergs: Lindsey, Cindy, Dad, and Justin. On following page: Pivoting on the double play can be tougher than combat duty.

PHOTOS BY STEPHEN GREEN

At left: Jim Frey gave me the confidence to swing for the fences. At right: The biggest difference between playing shortstop and second base is the way you have to make the throw to first.

their infield all set. Manny Trillo was at second base. Todd Cruz was at shortstop. Those were my two positions. So I didn't get a lot of playing time. But just the fact I was playing all year round helped me out, because the next year in Double A ball I had a good season. Then I went to Venezuela after the Double A season and followed that up with a good year at Triple A. I was staying sharp all year round.

I felt comfortable playing in the minors and felt that I was a pretty good minor league player. But I thought I was a long way from becoming an everyday big league player. That was another world to me. I think I learned a lot more about the mechanics of baseball once I got into pro ball. In high school, my coach taught me more about responsibility and being a team player.

The one guy who really stands out in my mind in the minor leagues in the Phillies organization was Larry Rojas. He was my Rookie Ball manager in Helena. He taught me so much that first year. After that, he became the traveling infield instructor for the Phillies. So he was with me all along and he really taught me how to play the infield positions. He was at the Florida Instructional Leagues in the winters and he followed me playing winter ball in Venezuela. Although the Phillies were never looking at me as a major prospect because they had other guys in mind, Larry Rojas said I could play in the big leagues. He just told me to keep working hard.

Jim Frey was the first one to really work with me offensively. He just set my mind straight on what he wanted me to do. He didn't mind if I went up there and was aggressive and swung for extra-base hits. In the past, I had been told to hit the ball on the ground and use my speed all the time. He just gave me the confidence to swing for power. I had early success with it and I stuck with it all year.

Last winter they named my old high school athletic stadium after me. What an honor! Ryne Sandberg Stadium. Can you imagine that? I was able to see a lot of my old friends from the class of 1978. It meant something special to me to be recognized like that.

I really felt uncomfortable with all the attention I received in high school. Before the athletic events we would always have a pep rally and they'd ask the team captain to come up and speak. I'd just say something brief like, "Let's go!" and that would be it. Typical Sandberg, right? I guess that's

Your basic 6-4-3 double play. In 1984, that meant Bowa- to-me-to-Durham.

There's no place like Home Sweet Home.

just the way I am and probably always will be.

I was a pretty good student, a B-plus student, even though I didn't study too much. I spent most of my time on athletics. I didn't spend a whole lot of time trying to become a great chemistry student or anything like that because I knew I probably wouldn't use it in the future. Don't get me wrong, I think school is important. But at that time, I just wanted to concentrate on sports.

Just because I had a year like I did in 1984 with the Cubs, I'm not going to go around hollering about being MVP and all that. It's my nature to act pretty quiet anyway. Maybe I can lead by example that way.

It was very exciting to receive the

I use a 32-ounce, 34-inch bat to get maximum speed in my swing.

MVP award, but I know that without my teammates—top players such as Gary Matthews, Jody Davis, Larry Bowa, Leon Durham, Ron Cey, Keith Moreland, and Bobby Dernier, along with our excellent pitching staff—I would not have been singled out for the recognition I received.

I feel more comfortable this year. I know what I can do defensively and offensively. I know what kind of player I can be. All I want to do is show consistent defense as I have the last two years and try to stay consistent with the bat. The power last year just came along because of consistency. The thing that surprised me the most was my ability to hit .300 so early in my career. And I know I'm going to have to work to maintain that level.

PHOTO BY STEPHEN GREEN

There's no substitute for speed on the bases.

The toughest play for a second baseman to make is when the ball goes to his right, up the middle. I try to make the backhand stop, plant my feet, and throw to first.

RYNO!

The one question people seemed to ask me the most over the winter and during spring training was about that June 23rd game against the Cardinals. I went 5-for-6 at the plate and knocked in seven runs. I hit two home runs off Bruce Sutter to keep us alive in the extra-inning game. But, most importantly, we won the game, 12–11 in 11 innings at Wrigley Field.

You don't even dream of getting five out of six hits with seven RBIs and two home runs. It just happened. That made me—and many others—believe that 1984 was going to be our year, and **my** year to make something special happen. It was definitely one of the biggest individual games that I have played in. I had two home runs in a game one time in high school, but it

Infield practice before the game helps me get loose and mentally prepared.

wasn't nearly as dramatic as this.

Facing Sutter, I wasn't thinking about hitting home runs. First of all, you've got one of the top relievers in the game on the mound. It's tough enough just to get a hit off of him. The first home run I hit in the ninth inning, I just swung the bat, and the ball went out. The second homer was like an instant replay of the first one. It was the first pitch, and it was up a little bit. Sometimes it pays off not to think when you go up to the plate; just swing the bat and let it happen.

Sutter basically throws one pitch, a split-fingered fastball that goes down and inside to a right-handed hitter. So I went up there looking for that pitch, thinking I was going to swing at the first strike he threw me so I wouldn't get in the hole. I think he was just trying to throw a strike and get-ahead

of me. Well, that day the wind was blowing out pretty good and any ball that was hit decently in the air was going to go out. So I knew it was gone as soon as I hit it. I didn't even know what to do when I was running around the bases. It was like running around on a cloud.

I remember that I felt confident coming to the plate for those last two homers. I was aware that I already had three hits and three RBIs, and the team was playing well. That might have had a lot to do with my approach to betting against Sutter. You have to have confidence and you have to be aggressive when you hit. That particular day, I got out of the chute early.

After the game, I really didn't realize what I had done. I was in shock. I remember saying I didn't even

PHOTO BY STEPHEN GREEN

No matter what city we're playing, there are no better fans in the world than those at Wrigley.

I've got one eye on the pitcher, and the other on third base coach Don Zimmer. I'm ready to go.

know what day it was. All the ingredients: a nationally televised game, a great pitcher on the mound, Wrigley Field . . . it was a great thrill for me.

That game gave me a lot of confidence and showed I could do something exceptional. I had always been labeled a player who was fundamentally sound, but did not do anything particularly extraordinary.

I got a lot of attention from friends and family the next week after the game. Family, distant relatives, and people I had never heard of who said they were my relatives all called to say they had seen that ball game. A lot of fans, even St. Louis fans that I ran into later, said "Thanks a lot. That was one of the greatest games I have ever seen." I got a lot of nice comments like that and it made me feel great.

I remember reading in the paper about the St. Louis manager, Whitey Herzog, calling me "The greatest player he had ever seen." He also referred to me as "Baby Ruth." Quite a compliment. I've always thought of him as being a great manager. I watched him on television as I was growing up. He's seen a lot of ball players. And when he says something like that, I didn't know what to think. But it was only halfway through the year. I said to myself: "Boy, I'd better keep it up. I don't want to let him down."

The fans in Chicago began saying that I should be the All-Star second baseman for the National League. At that time, I was a distant third in the voting and a week after that game I

took over the lead, and it was obvious to me that that game had a lot to do with it. I had done something special and different in a nationally televised game. I'll never forget the support the fans gave me in the All-Star voting. It was a great feeling.

In the past, I have always hit well when the weather has gotten hot. I like to get loose and sweat a little bit and then just let the natural ability take over. In May of 1984, I hit over .350. That happened to be the month Justin, my son, was born. I was on cloud nine and I wasn't thinking about anything but getting home to see Justin after the ball game every day. I was getting three hits a game. I was named Player of the Week the week after Justin was born. Having a child in the middle of the season like that takes a lot of pressure off you. It got me to relax. I

My first child, daughter Lindsey. Holding her wasn't any routine play—no room for an error here.

wasn't thinking about baseball that much.

One more thing about the '84 season: it didn't quite end the way I would have liked. All of the awards and honors are great, but the most important goal is helping your team to win a World Series. We almost made it, winning the National League East Division championship and the first two games of the playoffs against San Diego. But it just wasn't meant for us to win the pennant in 1984, it seems. So I want to do my part to get back in the playoffs. That challenge is what keeps me going in 1985.

◆   ◆   ◆

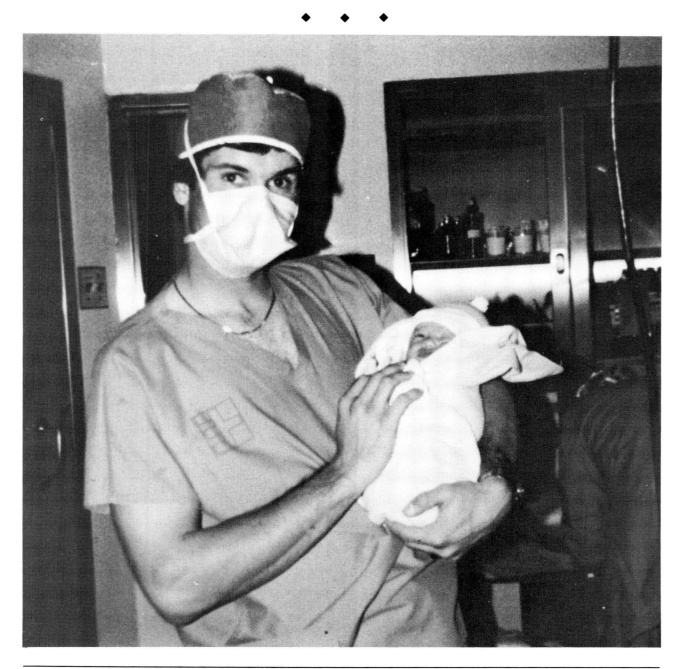

It's a boy! Justin was a big hit right off the bat at our house.

Hitting two home runs in one game off of Bruce Sutter is something I'll never, ever forget.

CHAPTER FIVE

THE 1985 CUBS

Many fans want to know about the 1985 Cubs, whether we are overconfident after winning the divisional title, whether we all get along well with one another. Well, I can say from my standpoint that I get along with all my teammates both on and off the field. They're just a great group of guys. And we are all professional enough to realize that we cannot approach the season overconfidently. It's tough enough for a team to repeat as champions in a division, without the players being overly optimistic.

That is not to say that there aren't periods of individual unrest and uneasiness. That's going to happen on any team and it is not necessarily a bad sign. It can happen in anything you do in life and there's no way to prevent it.

A controversy was stirred up during spring training between Larry Bowa and our third base coach, Don Zimmer. That confrontation was brewing for a long time. Zimmer accused Larry of being a selfish player and said that Larry refused to speak to me for a week to ten days during last season because he was jealous of me.

I think Larry was just going through a tough period then and didn't speak to anybody—his wife, his teammates, anybody. I know Larry is a tough and proud competitor who always wants to do his best on the field. I didn't take his actions personally, because I have a lot of respect for him.

If anything, this ball club is obsessed

I felt like I was running on a cloud when I hit that second home run off Sutter last June in that 12-11 win over the Cardinals.

RYNO!

At top: You have to be prepared to brave the elements at Wrigley Field—namely the wind and the sun. At bottom: Conditioning is one of the most important fundamentals for any athlete. You could say I'm getting a leg up on the competition.

with the idea of showing people that 1984 was no fluke. Many of us started out the 1985 season slowly at the plate, including me, but we all know that it is a very long season and just as the excellent pitching carried us the first few months of the season, I figure the hitters will pick up the slack later.

I'm swinging the same type of bat that I used last year—34 inches long and 32 ounces. I figure I can get around on a fastball pretty well with a light bat and I don't have to choke up. With as much hitting as we do in a game and during batting practice, I must go through three pairs of hitting gloves a week. Easily.

A good example of how this ball club gets along is the fact that we tolerate each other's music. Guys like Keith Moreland, Jody Davis, and Gary Woods like country music blaring in the locker room. Leon Durham, Lee Smith, and Thad Bosley go for the rhythm and blues. Younger guys like Bobby Dernier and I like rock and roll music—maybe Bruce Springsteen or Foreigner. And no matter what is playing, Richie Hebner wants to hear somebody like Roger Whittaker. It usually comes down to whoever can play his tape the loudest, and the rest of us have to learn to appreciate what's playing.

PHOTOS BY STEPHEN GREEN

At left: I'm just trying to keep the Cubs in the running for another division championship. At right: Flying spikes are an occupational hazard of being a second baseman. On following page: Mike Marshall is out at second, and I'm trying for a double play.

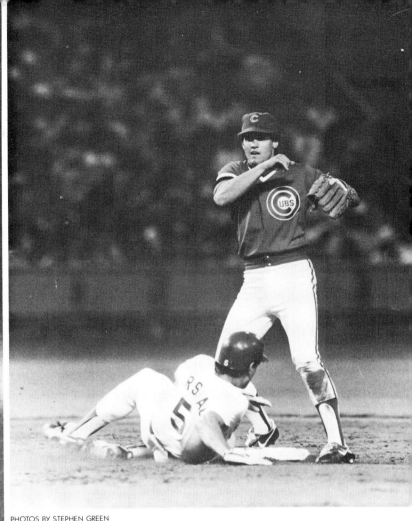

PHOTOS BY STEPHEN GREEN

RYNO!

Top left: Scoring runs is the name of the game, but I can see third base coach Don Zimmer telling me to hold up. Top right: Don't mess with me now, I've got Jody on my side. At bottom: One away from another Cub victory.

At top: The hand is quicker than the glove—but hopefully not when **I'm** wearing the glove.
At bottom: Everyone wants to take a swipe at the defending champs, especially the Phillies.

57

RYNO!

When I get on base, I know I can count on my teammates to drive me in.

The baseball experts say we should stomp on the Phillies this year. I hope they're right.

I feel like I'm in the best shape of my career, ready to run, slide, and hit home runs.

RYNO!

Regardless of who's playing next to me at shortstop—Shawon Dunston, Larry Bowa, or Chris Speier—our infield ranks with the best in baseball.

Keith Moreland (left) and Jody Davis are arguing over who's going to drive me in.

RYNO!

I learned how to play this card game called "Tonk" when I joined the Cubs, and that has helped me feel like "one of the guys." Bowa thinks he's pretty good at it and no matter what happens when we're playing, Ron Cey thinks he's always right. Billy Connors, the pitching coach, and Hebner usually play cribbage. There is always a lot of yelling and shouting and accusing that goes on in the game, but I guess that just means we're all having a good time.

And through all the apparent chaos in the clubhouse, Yosh Kawano, the equipment manager, keeps us in line.

Our coaches—Don Zimmer, John Vukovich, and Ruben Amaro—spend many hours with us, hitting ground balls and helping us position ourselves correctly for opposing batters. It is truly a team effort.

I have never been with a team like the Cubs, from the standpoint of everyone getting along and bringing out the best in one another. I'm not

saying there aren't disagreements or harsh words said at times, but it is all intended to help the team win. And once something is said, all is forgotten the next day.

The first few months of the 1985 season I could tell that pitchers were pitching me a little tougher than last year. But, by the same token, I think that umpires generally tend to give me the benefit of the doubt on close calls at the plate and in the field. I think that might be a benefit of winning the

Most Valuable Player Award.

The disappointment of not advancing to the World Series last fall has not yet healed, but we are motivated and dedicated to working harder in 1985 to make that dream become a reality.

For some reason, I have a very good feeling about the 1985 season. I think the fans will be in for another dramatic and exciting summer and a climactic fall. I know that I will be trying to do my part to make that happen.

◆ ◆ ◆

PHOTO BY STEPHEN GREEN

We're aiming to gun down the Padres this season.

ABOUT RYNO
BY FRED MITCHELL

RYNE DEE SANDBERG
HEIGHT: 6′2″
WEIGHT: 180 pounds

When Ryne Sandberg was named Most Valuable Player in the National League in 1984, he became the first Chicago Cub to win the award since Ernie Banks won it for a second straight time in 1959. Sandberg became only the fifth Cub in history to win MVP honors. The other four include catcher Gabby Hartnett in 1935, first baseman Phil Cavarretta in 1945, outfielder Hank Sauer in 1952, and Hall of Fame shortstop Banks in 1958 and 1959.

Sandberg, who was 24 years old throughout most of the 1984 season, won the MVP award in only his third full major-league campaign. Thus, he became the second youngest infielder ever to win the award. Ken Boyer was 23 years old when he won the MVP award in 1964 with the St. Louis Cardinals.

Sandberg was both spectacular and consistent at the plate and in the field in 1984. "No player has ever played as well for as long as Ryne did this season," praised Cubs manager Jim Frey.

Sandberg hit .314 in 156 games, the fourth best mark in the National League. His 200 hits were second only to batting champion Tony Gwynn of the San Diego Padres, who had 213 hits for a .351 average. Sandberg, who was the National League's starting second baseman in the 1984 All-Star Game, led the league in runs scored (114) and tied Juan Samuel of Philadelphia for the top spot with 19 triples. Sandberg also tied Samuel for

---

I'm reaching for another banner year in 1985. You can never be content with past accomplishments; you have to strive to reach new heights.

RYNO!

I don't like to choke up anymore; I feel that I'm strong enough to drive the ball to any field.

PHOTO BY STEPHEN GREEN

Things are looking up for the Cubs in '85.

RYNO!

third place in the NL with 36 doubles. Ryno's .520 slugging percentage was third behind top sluggers Dale Murphy of Atlanta (.547) and Mike Schmidt of Philadelphia (.536).

As a home-run hitter, Sandberg enjoyed his best year as a professional, smashing 19 homers. That was the most home runs hit by a Cubs second baseman since Rogers Hornsby blasted 40 in 1929.

Sandberg became the first Cubs second baseman since Billy Herman to have more than 70 extra-base hits in a season. He narrowly missed becoming the first player in major league history to collect 200 or more hits and 20 or more homers, triples, doubles, and

Ryne Sandberg—1984 National League MVP.

stolen bases in the same season. He missed by one home run and one triple.

On the base paths, Sandberg stole 32 bases, second to club leader and lead-off hitter Bobby Dernier (45). However, Sandberg had a better success ratio than Dernier, swiping 32 of 39, 82 percent.

The month of June was spectacular for Sandberg. He hit .376 (47 for 125), scored 27 runs, had 21 RBIs, seven doubles, six triples, eight home runs, and six stolen bases. He also had a superior month in August, batting .366 (34 for 91) with a 15-game hitting streak during which he batted .383.

Earlier in the '84 season Sandberg had an 18-game hitting streak, which turned out to be the longest on the club. That streak went from April 24

This award meant at lot, but I would have traded it in for one more playoff win.

RYNO!

to May 16, during which time he batted .421 (32 for 76) and had 10 multi-hit games.

In postseason play Ryno batted .368 against San Diego. He went 7 for 19 and collected a hit in each of the five games. He had two hits in games 1 and 2, played in Chicago, along with two RBIs.

Defensively, Sandberg earned his second straight Gold Glove in 1984, committing only six errors in 156 games. In 1983, he had become the first player in the NL to win a Gold Glove in his first year at a new position, after playing third base in 1982.

During a 61-game stretch from June

29 through September 6 of 1984, Sandberg did not commit a single error. That was the longest errorless streak by a second baseman in the NL in 1984.

Sandberg finished with a fielding percentage of .9932, just missing the all-time NL record by a second baseman, held by Manny Trillo, who had a fielding mark of .9937 with the Philadelphia Phillies in 1982. In 1983, when he won the Gold Glove, Sandberg had made only 13 errors and finished with a percentage of .986.

Sandberg came to the Cubs along with shortstop Larry Bowa on January 27, 1982, in a trade with the Phillies for shortstop Ivan DeJesus. In his first

Collecting 200 hits last season was a special goal for me. I'm striving for consistency at the plate every year.

A second baseman always has to be alert for pickoff throws from the catcher.

RYNO!

season with the Cubs, Sandberg was selected Chicago Rookie of the Year by the Chicago chapter of the Baseball Writers of America.

After a 1-for-32 start at the plate in 1982, Sandberg finished with a solid .271 batting average. He was second on the Cubs in doubles (33) and stolen bases (32) and led the club in runs scored with 103. The 103 runs scored set a club record for a rookie, eclipsing the 50-year-old mark held by Billy Herman. Ryno's 32 stolen bases were also a club record for a third baseman, erasing Harry Steinfeldt's mark of 29, set in 1906.

Adjusting to a new position at second base in 1983, Sandberg's average dropped to .261. He had 25 doubles, four triples, eight homers, and 48 runs in 1983.

He nearly doubled his RBI total in 1984. He knocked in seven runs in one game against the St. Louis Cardinals on June 23. He went 5 for 6 that day, with two homers in a nationally televised game. The dramatic homers both came against St. Louis ace reliever Bruce Sutter and helped the Cubs win a pulsating 12–11 contest at Wrigley Field in 11 innings. Afterwards, St. Louis manager Whitey Herzog called Sandberg "the greatest player I have ever seen."

Here is a chart illustrating the balloting for the 1984 National League Most Valuable Player (top 10 players):

NAME	FIRST-PLACE VOTES	TOTAL
Ryne Sandberg, Cubs	22	326
Keith Hernandez, Mets	1	195
Tony Gwynn, Padres	1	184
Rick Sutcliffe, Cubs	0	151
Gary Matthews, Cubs	0	70
Bruce Sutter, Cards	0	67
Mike Schmidt, Phillies	0	55.5
Jose Cruz, Astros	0	53.5
Dale Murphy, Braves	0	52.5
Jody Davis, Cubs	0	49

Here is a month-by-month breakdown of Sandberg's 1984 MVP season:

MONTH	AVG.	AB	H	HR	RBIs
April	.259	81	21	2	14
May	.373	110	41	1	16
June	.376	125	47	8	21
July	.292	113	33	3	13
August	.366	93	34	4	9
September	.255	94	24	1	11

With Leon Durham at first base, I'm always confident that we'll make the double play.